PHOTO FUN PICTURE PUZZLES

ANIMALS

THUNDER BAY
P · R · E · S · S
San Diego, California

Thunder Bay Press
An imprint of the Baker & Taylor Publishing Group
10350 Barnes Canyon Road, San Diego, CA 92121
www.thunderbaybooks.com

Copyright © Thunder Bay, 2011

Design, layout, and photo manipulation by
quadrum■
www.quadrumltd.com

ISBN-13: 978-1-60710-225-0
ISBN-10: 1-60710-225-0

Printed in India.

Contents

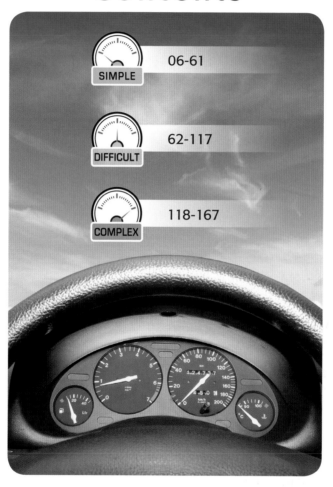

SPOT THE USAGE

Types of puzzles

The book has three types of puzzles with one, two, or eight pictures on every page. Each puzzle may have five to ten differences, or an odd image that you have to spot.

ONE PICTURE PER PAGE

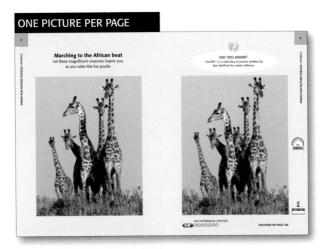

Compare the pictures on two opposite pages and spot the differences between them.

TWO PICTURES PER PAGE

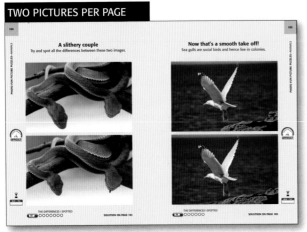

Compare two pictures on the same page and spot the differences between them.

EIGHT PICTURES PER PAGE

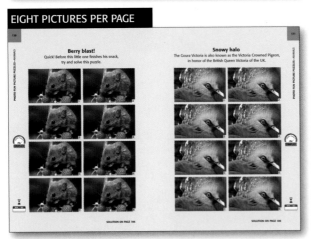

Look at all the eight pictures on the same page and spot the odd one out.

Symbols used

1

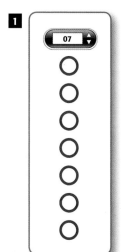

Tick off a circle for every difference you find.

2

DID YOU KNOW?
Studies have proved that happy people live longer, make more money, and receive better job reviews.

Included is a "Did You Know" fact to keep you interested as you go about spotting the differences!

3

SOLUTIONS ON PAGE 100

Help is close at hand. Just turn to the right page to see the answers.

4

Record the time you take to find all the differences.

Difficulty meters

The sections are color coded to be in line with the difficulty meter. This is helpful in identifying the level of complexity of each puzzle. See how far you can push yourself!

SIMPLE

DIFFICULT

COMPLEX

Marching to the African beat
Let these magnificent creatures inspire you,
as you solve this fun puzzle.

DID YOU KNOW?
*"Giraffe" is a collection of poems written by
Don Mulford for senior citizens.*

SIMPLE

MIN : SEC

THE DIFFERENCES I SPOTTED

07 ○○○○○○○

SOLUTION ON PAGE 168

Let us part ways
Find the differences between these two images.

SIMPLE

MIN : SEC

THE DIFFERENCES I SPOTTED

08 ⬍ ○○○○○○○○

SOLUTION ON PAGE 168

Gliding along
You may not have eight arms to help you,
but solve this puzzle as quickly as you can.

SIMPLE

MIN : SEC

THE DIFFERENCES I SPOTTED

06 ○○○○○○

SOLUTION ON PAGE 168

Best view in the house

These images may seem as though they have the same view,
but there are many differences. Try and spot all seven of them.

SIMPLE

MIN : SEC

THE DIFFERENCES I SPOTTED

10 ○○○○○○○○○○

SOLUTION ON PAGE 168

Because she cares

"God could not be everywhere and therefore he made mothers."
— Unknown Source

SIMPLE

MIN : SEC

THE DIFFERENCES I SPOTTED

05 ○○○○○

SOLUTION ON PAGE 168

Leap of faith

Horse jumping was popularized by the English in the eighteenth century, when they had to jump fences on their fox hunts.

SIMPLE

MIN : SEC

THE DIFFERENCES I SPOTTED

08 ○○○○○○○○

SOLUTION ON PAGE 168

A tub of puppies
Add to the fun. Solve this puzzle against the clock.

SIMPLE

MIN : SEC

THE DIFFERENCES I SPOTTED

06 ○○○○○○

SOLUTION ON PAGE 169

Have you any wool?
The ratio of sheep to man in New Zealand in 2005 was 12:1.

SIMPLE

MIN : SEC

THE DIFFERENCES I SPOTTED

06 ○○○○○○

SOLUTION ON PAGE 169

Follow me into the deep blue

Concentrate on the pristine and discover all the differences between the two images.

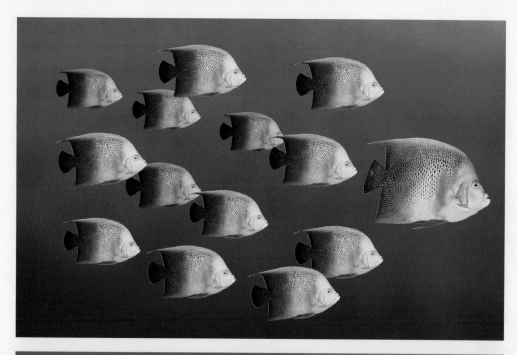

SIMPLE

MIN : SEC

THE DIFFERENCES I SPOTTED

06 ○○○○○○

SOLUTION ON PAGE 169

Curled and cozy

Green Snake (1993) is a Hong Kong–based fantasy film adapted from the novel by Lillian Lee.

SIMPLE

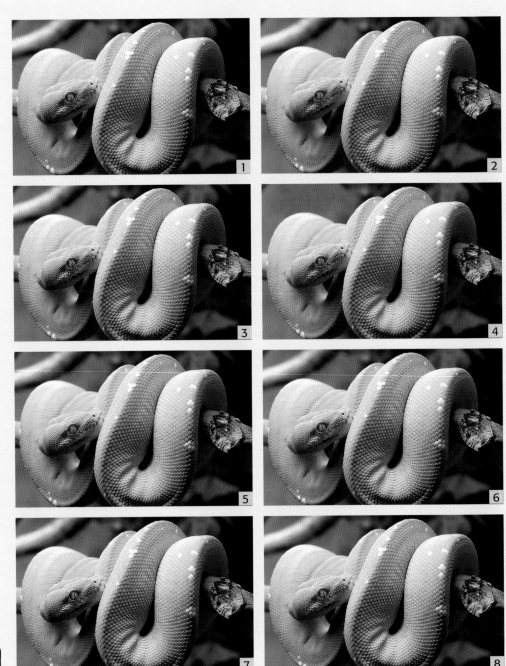

MIN : SEC

SOLUTION ON PAGE 169

Waiting for my princess
Tree frogs descend from the trees only during mating season,
or under exceptional circumstances.

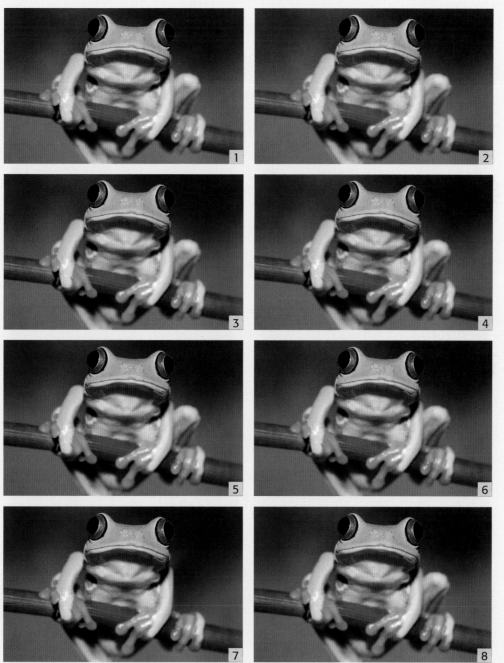

SIMPLE

MIN : SEC

SOLUTION ON PAGE 169

The king of camouflage

There are approximately 160 species of chameleon throughout the world–from Hawaii in America, to Sri Lanka in Asia, and Madagascar in Africa.

SIMPLE

MIN : SEC

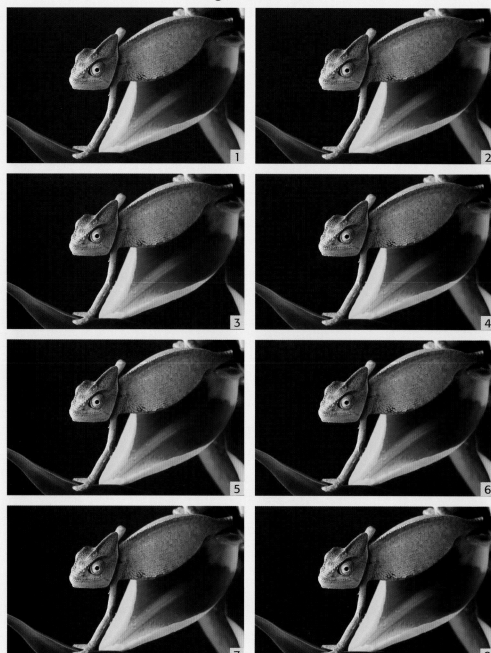

SOLUTION ON PAGE 169

An exotic couple

All these colorful images may look the same, but there is an odd one. Try and spot it.

SIMPLE

MIN : SEC

SOLUTION ON PAGE 170

The best ski resort

Just like these cute fellows, you too can have a jolly time.
Sit back, relax, and have a great time solving this puzzle.

DID YOU KNOW?
During breeding season, which occurs in October, there is a penguin safari in Snow Hill Island, Antarctica.

SIMPLE

MIN : SEC

THE DIFFERENCES I SPOTTED

07 ○○○○○○○

SOLUTION ON PAGE 170

My koala bear

These cute tree-hugging bears are solitary animals, and therefore, are never found in packs.

SIMPLE

MIN : SEC

THE DIFFERENCES I SPOTTED

05 ⬍ ○○○○○

SOLUTION ON PAGE 170

Hanging around

Leopards are solitary animals. They are seldom seen interacting apart from mating or rearing their young.

SIMPLE

MIN : SEC

THE DIFFERENCES I SPOTTED

07 ◯◯◯◯◯◯◯

SOLUTION ON PAGE 170

Our favorite couple

As quickly as possible, try and spot all the differences between these images.

SIMPLE

MIN : SEC

THE DIFFERENCES I SPOTTED

07 ○○○○○○○

SOLUTION ON PAGE 170

We'll stare you down

Lemurs derive their name from the "lemure" of Roman mythology, which means ghost or spirit.

SIMPLE

MIN : SEC

THE DIFFERENCES I SPOTTED

07 ○○○○○○○

SOLUTION ON PAGE 170

When passion and power collide

It is the mare that plays the role of leader in the herd and is often referred to as the "boss mare."

SIMPLE

MIN : SEC

THE DIFFERENCES I SPOTTED

06 ○○○○○○

SOLUTION ON PAGE 171

This print suits me best

The cheetah is one of the four cats that has semi-retractable claws. Others being the fishing cat, flat-headed cat, and the Iriomote cat.

SIMPLE

MIN : SEC

THE DIFFERENCES I SPOTTED

SOLUTION ON PAGE 171

A pair that helps

The donkey belongs to the "Equidae" or horse family.
A male donkey is called jack and the female jenny.

SIMPLE

MIN : SEC

THE DIFFERENCES I SPOTTED

08 ○○○○○○○○

SOLUTION ON PAGE 100

The perfect day

Before the cows are finished grazing, try and spot all the differences between these two images.

SIMPLE

MIN : SEC

THE DIFFERENCES I SPOTTED

SOLUTION ON PAGE 100

Let's see what's out there
Solve this pretty puzzle as quickly as possible and beat the clock!

SIMPLE

MIN : SEC

SOLUTION ON PAGE 171

The power of love
"Soul meets soul on lovers' lips." — Percy Shelley

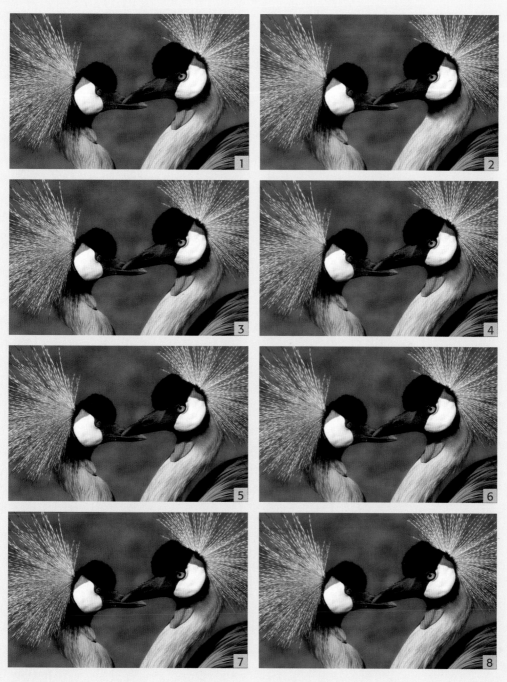

SIMPLE

MIN : SEC

SOLUTION ON PAGE PAGE 171

Free Willy

Keiko is the name of the orca that plays the role of Willy
in the film *Free Willy*.

SIMPLE

MIN : SEC

SOLUTION ON PAGE 172

I'm not always crabby!

The Sally Lightfoot crab, at birth, is almost completely black and gains color as it matures.

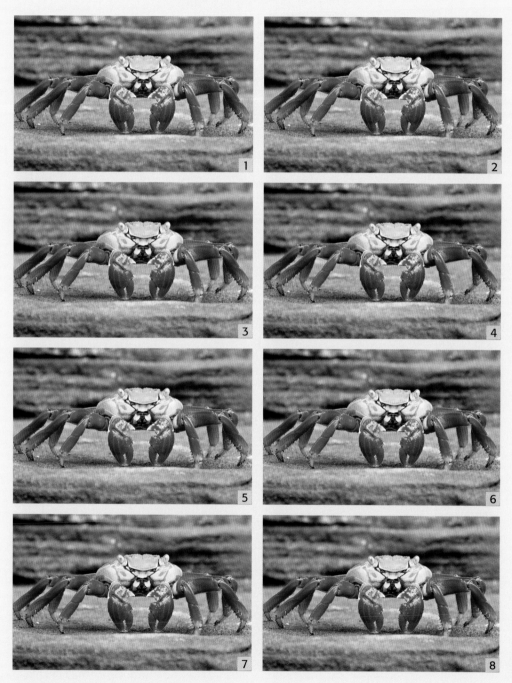

SIMPLE

MIN : SEC

SOLUTION ON PAGE 172

Wide-eyed and watching

If you look carefully, you will be able to find all the differences between these two images.

DID YOU KNOW?
The average life of a ring-tailed lemur is 18 years in the wild and 25 years in captivity.

SIMPLE

MIN : SEC

THE DIFFERENCES I SPOTTED

 06 ○○○○○○

SOLUTION ON PAGE 172

Thirst-quenching!
Sip on a refreshing drink as you try and solve this puzzle.

SIMPLE

MIN : SEC

THE DIFFERENCES I SPOTTED

`06` ○○○○○○

SOLUTION ON PAGE 172

We love the sun as well!

Like these tortoises, you too could go outdoors and enjoy the sun as you solve this puzzle.

SIMPLE

MIN : SEC

THE DIFFERENCES I SPOTTED

08 ○○○○○○○○

SOLUTION ON PAGE 172

Our favorite watering hole

Taking inspiration from these wise, gentle giants, see if you can find all the differences between these two images.

SIMPLE

MIN : SEC

THE DIFFERENCES I SPOTTED

07 ◇ ○○○○○○○

SOLUTION ON PAGE 172

Some picnic fun
Try and solve this puzzle before the round is over.

SIMPLE

MIN : SEC

THE DIFFERENCES I SPOTTED

SOLUTION ON PAGE 173

Pink is the new black

In tenth century BC, flamingo tongue was considered an excellent delicacy by Romans.

SIMPLE

MIN : SEC

THE DIFFERENCES I SPOTTED

09 ○○○○○○○○○

SOLUTION ON PAGE 173

The furry pack

This pack is on the prowl for some fun.
Help them by solving the puzzle.

SIMPLE

MIN : SEC

THE DIFFERENCES I SPOTTED

08 ⟳ ○○○○○○○○

SOLUTION ON PAGE 173

My home goes where I go

Mediterranean Tortoise is the common name for a group of tortoises that includes the spur-thighed tortoise and the Hermann's Tortoise.

SIMPLE

MIN : SEC

SOLUTION ON PAGE 173

Aflame with color

The life expectancy of flamingoes is one of the longest in birds,
as they can live up to the age of forty.

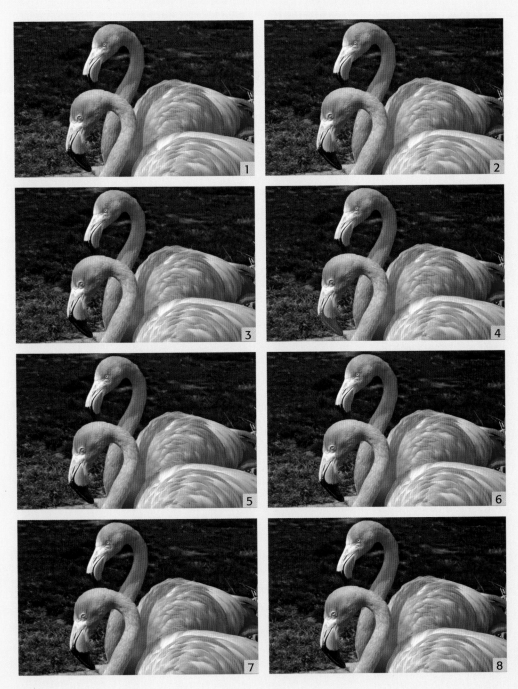

SIMPLE

MIN : SEC

SOLUTION ON PAGE 173

Sharing is caring

Before the squirrel changes his mind, try and find the odd one out.

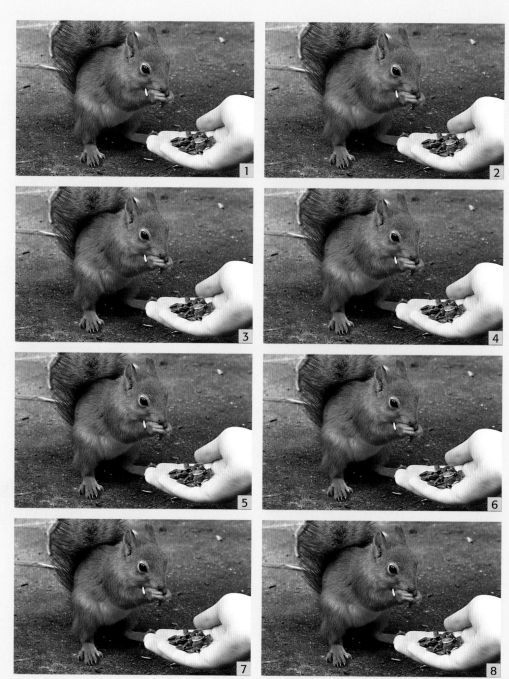

SIMPLE

MIN : SEC

SOLUTION ON PAGE 173

Snack time

Can't decide which is more beautiful? That's okay, because to solve this puzzle you only have to spot the odd image.

SIMPLE

MIN : SEC

SOLUTION ON PAGE 174

My first tricycle

Before this little pup progresses to a bicycle, try and spot all the differences between these two images.

DID YOU KNOW?
Pugs originate from China. They were popularized in Western Europe by the House of Orange of the Netherlands.

SIMPLE

MIN : SEC

THE DIFFERENCES I SPOTTED

09 ○○○○○○○○○

SOLUTION ON PAGE 174

Three's company

In sixteenth century, people of England believed that the Cavalier King Charles Spaniel could cure stomach ailments, and was popularly known as "comforters."

SIMPLE

MIN : SEC

THE DIFFERENCES I SPOTTED

06 ○○○○○○

SOLUTION ON PAGE 174

Running like the wind

In Greek mythology, it is believed that the white-winged horse was the son of Medusa and Poseidon, and that Poseidon was the creator of horses.

SIMPLE

MIN : SEC

THE DIFFERENCES I SPOTTED

 06 ○○○○○○

SOLUTION ON PAGE 174

Happy as a duck in water

"Be like a duck. Calm on the surface, but always paddling like the dickens underneath." — Michael Caine

SIMPLE

MIN : SEC

THE DIFFERENCES I SPOTTED

06 ○○○○○○

SOLUTION ON PAGE 174

Family picnic

"A happy family is but an earlier heaven." — John Bowring

SIMPLE

MIN : SEC

THE DIFFERENCES I SPOTTED

SOLUTION ON PAGE 174

Odd one out

Due to deforestation, a majority of macaws are on the endangered species list. The Spix and Glauccous macaws are considered nearly extinct.

SIMPLE

MIN : SEC

THE DIFFERENCES I SPOTTED

07 ○○○○○○○

SOLUTION ON PAGE 175

Being wise is hard work
Slowly and steadily, try and solve this puzzle.

SIMPLE

MIN : SEC

THE DIFFERENCES I SPOTTED

07 ○○○○○○○

SOLUTION ON PAGE 175

The funniest caravan

The camels that are found in India have a single hump.

SIMPLE

MIN : SEC

THE DIFFERENCES I SPOTTED

07 ○○○○○○○

SOLUTION ON PAGE 175

Thanksgiving?

Since the year 1863, Thanksgiving has been annually observed in the United States.

SIMPLE

MIN : SEC

THE DIFFERENCES I SPOTTED

06 ○○○○○○

SOLUTION ON PAGE 175

Pretty in pink

Beat the clock! Try and spot all the differences between these two images as quickly as you can.

SIMPLE

MIN : SEC

THE DIFFERENCES I SPOTTED

07 ○○○○○○○

SOLUTION ON PAGE 175

On vacation until Christmas
While on a break, solve this fun puzzle!

SIMPLE

MIN : SEC

THE DIFFERENCES I SPOTTED

06 ○○○○○○

SOLUTION ON PAGE 175

Wild cat

Historically, the Royal Bengal Tiger is the largest subspecies, second largest only to the Siberian Tiger.

SIMPLE

MIN : SEC

THE DIFFERENCES I SPOTTED

07 ⬥ ◯◯◯◯◯◯◯

SOLUTION ON PAGE 176

Home is where I go

The Chinese consider the turtle to symbolize wisdom and patience.

SIMPLE

MIN : SEC

THE DIFFERENCES I SPOTTED

07

SOLUTION ON PAGE 176

Triumph of the will

This lot is very determined to reach their destination. Are you as determined to find all the differences between these two images?

DID YOU KNOW?
Calves of the wild bison are much lighter in color than a mature Bison. The rare white calf is considered sacred among Native Americans.

DIFFICULT

MIN : SEC

THE DIFFERENCES I SPOTTED

07 ⬍ ○○○○○○○

SOLUTION ON PAGE 176

A feathery bunch

Try and find all the differences between these images
and beat the clock.

DIFFICULT

MIN : SEC

THE DIFFERENCES I SPOTTED

07

SOLUTION ON PAGE 176

Round table conference

The meeting is in session. Before it concludes,
spot all the differences between the images.

DIFFICULT

MIN : SEC

THE DIFFERENCES I SPOTTED

08 ⟳ ○○○○○○○○

SOLUTION ON PAGE 176

I will swim with you into the deepest blue

"At the touch of love, everyone becomes a poet." — Plato

DIFFICULT

MIN : SEC

THE DIFFERENCES I SPOTTED

06 ○○○○○○

SOLUTION ON PAGE 176

I too have stripes to show off

Just as the caterpillar finds its way, see if you can find all the differences between the images.

DIFFICULT

MIN : SEC

THE DIFFERENCES I SPOTTED

SOLUTION ON PAGE 177

There's nothing as nice as hugging mom

"If you have a mom, there is nowhere you are likely to go where a prayer has not already been." — Robert Brault

DIFFICULT

MIN : SEC

THE DIFFERENCES I SPOTTED

06 ○○○○○○

SOLUTION ON PAGE 177

Dinnertime
Solve this puzzle as quickly as you can.

DIFFICULT

MIN : SEC

THE DIFFERENCES I SPOTTED

08 ⬦ ○○○○○○○○

SOLUTION ON PAGE 177

Lone wolf

The grey wolf is the largest wolf of the *Canidae* family. It is an apex predator, facing threats only from tigers and humans.

DIFFICULT

MIN : SEC

THE DIFFERENCES I SPOTTED

08 ○○○○○○○○

SOLUTION ON PAGE 177

Natural elegance

"Calm, white calm, was born into a swan." — Elizabeth Coatsworth

DIFFICULT

MIN : SEC

THE DIFFERENCES I SPOTTED

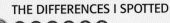 ○○○○○○

SOLUTION ON PAGE 177

A yellow horse!

Seahorses don't have scales but have bony plates under their skin that serves and looks like armor.

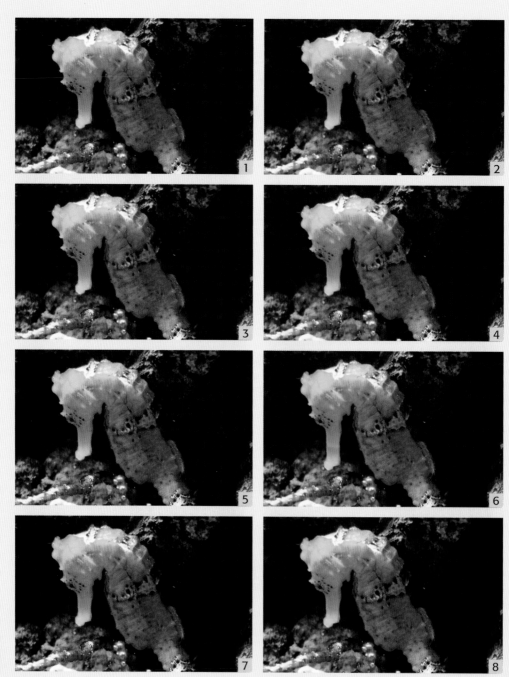

DIFFICULT

MIN : SEC

SOLUTION ON PAGE 177

Cock-a-doodle-doo

From this lot, there is an odd rooster. Can you find him as he is urgently needed to wake the other animals up?

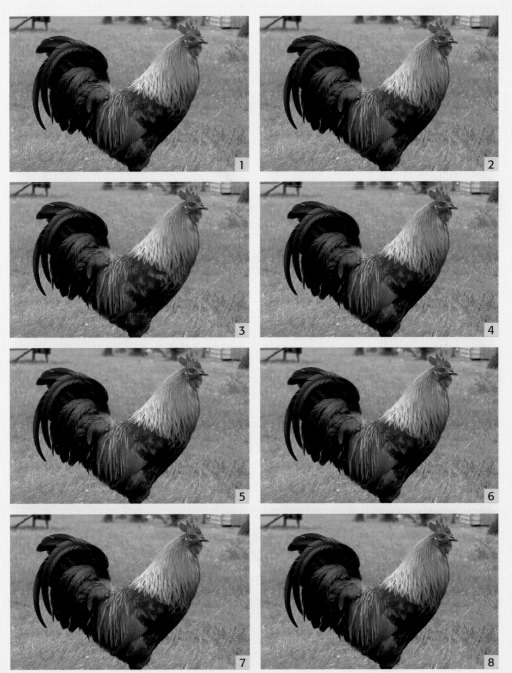

DIFFICULT

MIN : SEC

SOLUTION ON PAGE 178

Cuteness lined up

Try and beat the clock by finding all the differences between these two images as quickly as possible.

DID YOU KNOW?

Hounds are classified into three types: sight hounds, scent hounds, and "others," which is any hound that doesn't fall into the other categories.

DIFFICULT

MIN : SEC

THE DIFFERENCES I SPOTTED

SOLUTION ON PAGE 178

Flipper's day out
A bottle-nose dolphin can live upto fifty years.

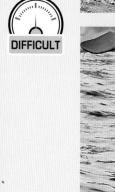

DIFFICULT

MIN : SEC

THE DIFFERENCES I SPOTTED

06 ○○○○○○

SOLUTION ON PAGE 178

You get all kinds

"A mere friend will agree with you but a real friend will argue."
— Russian proverb

DIFFICULT

MIN : SEC

THE DIFFERENCES I SPOTTED

06 ○○○○○○

SOLUTION ON PAGE 178

Friends always make everything pleasant

"A good friend remembers what we were and sees what we can be." — Unknown Source

DIFFICULT

MIN : SEC

THE DIFFERENCES I SPOTTED

08 ○○○○○○○○

SOLUTION ON PAGE 178

Sweater anyone?

Try and spot all the differences between these two images.

DIFFICULT

MIN : SEC

THE DIFFERENCES I SPOTTED

06 ○○○○○○

SOLUTION ON PAGE 178

Bear hug!
"You can't wrap love in a box, but you can wrap a person in a hug." — Unknown Source

DIFFICULT

MIN : SEC

THE DIFFERENCES I SPOTTED

06 ○○○○○○

SOLUTION ON PAGE 179

Nature never ceases to amaze

Try and spot all the differences between these images
as quickly as you can.

DIFFICULT

MIN : SEC

THE DIFFERENCES I SPOTTED

07 ○○○○○○○

SOLUTION ON PAGE 179

I rule this roost

"What is more miraculous than an egg yolk turning into
a chicken?" — S. Parkes Cadman

DIFFICULT

MIN : SEC

THE DIFFERENCES I SPOTTED

06 ○○○○○○

SOLUTION ON PAGE 179

Count my spots

In the 1961 animated movie *101 Dalmatians*, the name of the cat that saves the 99 puppies from Cruella de Vil is Sergeant Tibbs.

DIFFICULT

MIN : SEC

THE DIFFERENCES I SPOTTED

 07

SOLUTION ON PAGE 179

I've got my eye on you
Found on the eastern side of South Africa, the Eastern Green
Mamba is the smallest member of the mamba family.

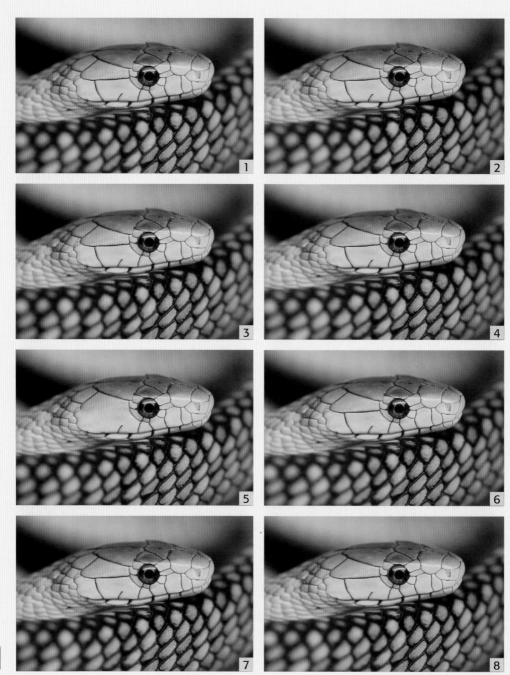

DIFFICULT

MIN : SEC

SOLUTION ON PAGE 179

Gliding along

Just like this little slug cruising about, solve this puzzle as quickly as you can and cruise to the next level.

DIFFICULT

MIN : SEC

SOLUTION ON PAGE 179

A cheerful pair
Before this pair decides to fly off, solve this puzzle.

DID YOU KNOW?

There are about 370 species of parrots in the world.

DIFFICULT

MIN : SEC

THE DIFFERENCES I SPOTTED

08 ⬦ ○○○○○○○○

SOLUTION ON PAGE 180

Success is a state of mind

With friends like this, anything is possible. Invite a friend to join you as you solve this puzzle to make it more enjoyable.

DIFFICULT

MIN : SEC

THE DIFFERENCES I SPOTTED

07 ○○○○○○○

SOLUTION ON PAGE 180

Cute and grumpy

Koala bears are found on the coastal region of Australia, between Adelaide and Cape York Peninsula.

DIFFICULT

MIN : SEC

THE DIFFERENCES I SPOTTED

06 ○○○○○○

SOLUTION ON PAGE 180

Up in the air

"Whenever you observe an animal closely, you feel as if a human being sitting inside were making fun of you." — Elias Canetti

DIFFICULT

MIN : SEC

THE DIFFERENCES I SPOTTED

09 ○○○○○○○○○

SOLUTION ON PAGE 180

Go green!

The Madagascar Day Gecko is a subspecies of geckos. It is found in rain forests and mainly dwells on trees.

DIFFICULT

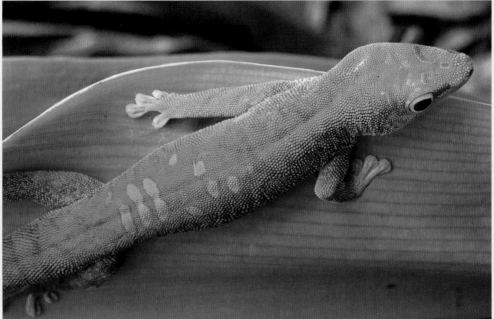

MIN : SEC

THE DIFFERENCES I SPOTTED

07 ○○○○○○○

SOLUTION ON PAGE 180

Three stooges

"Love will draw an elephant through a key-hole."
— Samuel Richardson

DIFFICULT

MIN : SEC

THE DIFFERENCES I SPOTTED

07 ○○○○○○○

SOLUTION ON PAGE 180

I need to test the waters first

In ancient times, the giraffe was associated to the *Qilin*, a mythical Chinese creature.

DIFFICULT

MIN : SEC

THE DIFFERENCES I SPOTTED

SOLUTION ON PAGE 181

Underwater tigers

These images might look quite similar, but there are seven differences. Try and spot them.

DIFFICULT

MIN : SEC

THE DIFFERENCES I SPOTTED

07 ○○○○○○○

SOLUTION ON PAGE 181

Nuts!
Squirrels are omnivores and are found in the regions of Asia, Europe, Africa, and America.

DIFFICULT

MIN : SEC

THE DIFFERENCES I SPOTTED

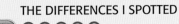

SOLUTION ON PAGE 181

It's that way. No, it's this way.

This couple, like most couples, is fuzzy about directions. As they figure out their way, can you figure which image is the odd one?

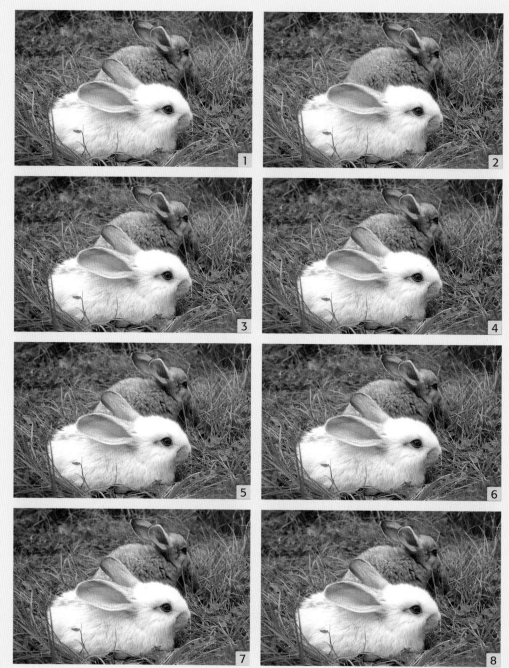

DIFFICULT

MIN : SEC

SOLUTION ON PAGE 181

Mom always knows exactly what to do
"Of all the rights of a woman, the greatest is to be a mother."
— Lin Yutang

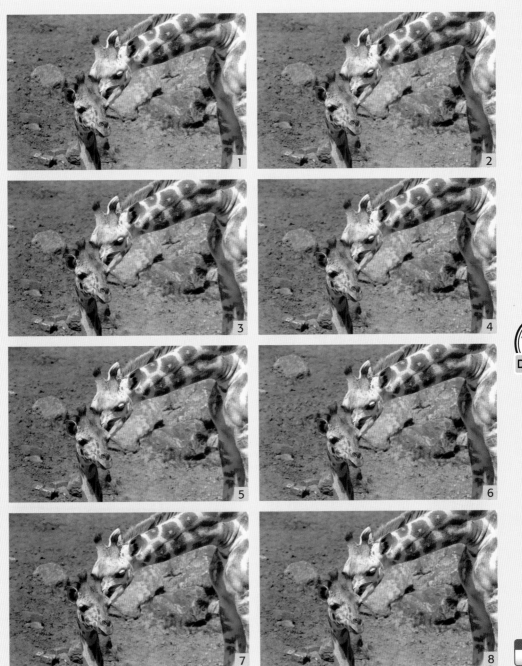

DIFFICULT

MIN : SEC

SOLUTION ON PAGE 181

The English countryside
Try and finish this puzzle in time for high tea.

DID YOU KNOW?
High tea is also known as "meat tea" as cold meats and eggs are served along with cakes and sandwiches–and of course the tea!

DIFFICULT

MIN : SEC

THE DIFFERENCES I SPOTTED

08 ○○○○○○○○

SOLUTION ON PAGE 181

Look at me

"It is not only fine feathers that make fine birds." — Aesop

DIFFICULT

MIN : SEC

THE DIFFERENCES I SPOTTED

06 ○○○○○○

SOLUTION ON PAGE 182

You looking at me?

The Kudu Antelope's horn is used as a musical instrument in many cultures. It is used often in Jewish ceremonies and is called a *shofar*.

DIFFICULT

MIN : SEC

THE DIFFERENCES I SPOTTED

07 ○○○○○○○

SOLUTION ON PAGE 182

A slithery couple

Try and spot all the differences between these two images.

DIFFICULT

MIN : SEC

THE DIFFERENCES I SPOTTED

07 ○○○○○○○

SOLUTION ON PAGE 182

Now that's a smooth take off!
Sea gulls are social birds and hence live in colonies.

DIFFICULT

MIN : SEC

THE DIFFERENCES I SPOTTED

SOLUTION ON PAGE 182

We share everything

Before this group of friends finishes their drink, try and find all the differences between the images.

DIFFICULT

MIN : SEC

THE DIFFERENCES I SPOTTED

07 ⬍ ○○○○○○○

SOLUTION ON PAGE 182

A family outing

The African elephant can easily be distinguished from the Indian elephant, as it is much larger in size and its ears are also bigger.

DIFFICULT

MIN : SEC

THE DIFFERENCES I SPOTTED

08 ○○○○○○○○

SOLUTION ON PAGE 182

Steady stroll

Before the turtle reaches its destination, try and find
all the differences between the images.

DIFFICULT

MIN : SEC

THE DIFFERENCES I SPOTTED

07 ○○○○○○○

SOLUTION ON PAGE 183

Beach bums at heart

Lion cubs are born with spots on their body, like that of leopards,
and with age these fade away.

DIFFICULT

MIN : SEC

THE DIFFERENCES I SPOTTED

08 ○○○○○○○○

SOLUTION ON PAGE 183

Honeylicious

Throughout history, from Shakespeare to Tolstoy, honeybee communities have been used to symbolize human society.

DIFFICULT

MIN : SEC

THE DIFFERENCES I SPOTTED
07 ○○○○○○○

SOLUTION ON PAGE 183

Who you calling a guinea pig?
Guinea pigs are commonly called cavies as they belong to the Cavidae rodent family.

DIFFICULT

MIN : SEC

THE DIFFERENCES I SPOTTED

05 ○○○○○

SOLUTION ON PAGE 183

Flames of the Caribbean

Try and solve this colorful puzzle as quickly as possible.

DIFFICULT

MIN : SEC

THE DIFFERENCES I SPOTTED

07 ○○○○○○○

SOLUTION ON PAGE 183

A sea of sheep

The first sheep to be brought to New Zealand was by Captain Cook in 1773. Currently, the sheep population there is 43.1 million.

DIFFICULT

MIN : SEC

THE DIFFERENCES I SPOTTED

SOLUTION ON PAGE 183

Man's Best Friend

Heterochromia, that is having different colored eyes,
is common among huskies.

DIFFICULT

MIN : SEC

SOLUTION ON PAGE 184

Yes, we look a lot alike

The Colobus monkeys are born completely white and will gain its black-and-white coloring around 3 months old.

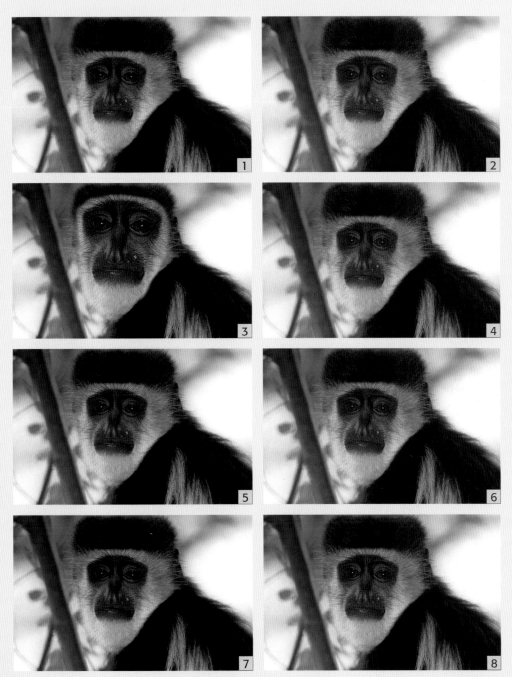

DIFFICULT

MIN : SEC

SOLUTION ON PAGE 184

Lost bunny
One of these bunnies is lost. Can you help find him?

DIFFICULT

MIN : SEC

SOLUTION ON PAGE 184

Do not disturb!

The shell of a box turtle has a hinge at the bottom, so that it can seal itself up and escape from predators.

DIFFICULT

MIN : SEC

SOLUTION ON PAGE 184

Fish sprinkles

Solving this puzzle may seem very complicated, but it's really
as fun as swimming through a coral reef.

DID YOU KNOW?
Coral reefs form some of the most diverse ecosystems of the planet and are therefore referred to as the rainforests of the sea.

COMPLEX

MIN : SEC

THE DIFFERENCES I SPOTTED

10 ○○○○○○○○○○

SOLUTION ON PAGE 184

Flamingo lagoon

Chilean flamingoes have gray legs but distinctly pink knees and large black bills. Young chicks lack color and are mostly gray all over.

COMPLEX

MIN : SEC

THE DIFFERENCES I SPOTTED

09 ○○○○○○○○○

SOLUTION ON PAGE 184

Cool cat
Andrew Lloyd Webber's musical *Cats* is based on T. S. Eliot's
Old Possum's Book of Practical Cats.

COMPLEX

MIN : SEC

THE DIFFERENCES I SPOTTED

08 ○○○○○○○○

SOLUTION ON PAGE 185

The grass is greener

Optimism makes for a great companion. Don't give up until you find all the differences between these two images.

COMPLEX

MIN : SEC

THE DIFFERENCES I SPOTTED

08 ○○○○○○○○

SOLUTION ON PAGE 185

Teamwork pays

Make this puzzle even more fun, by asking a friend
to help you solve it!

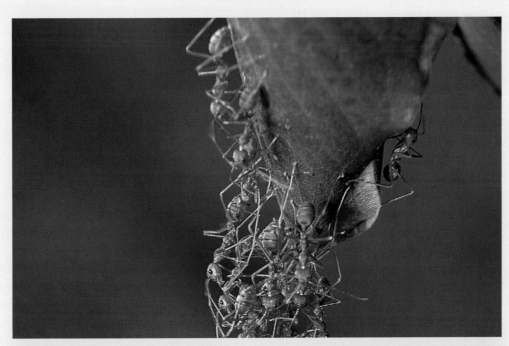

COMPLEX

MIN : SEC

THE DIFFERENCES I SPOTTED

06 ○○○○○○

SOLUTION ON PAGE 185

Moove over

Without getting lost in the English countryside, try and find all the differences between these images.

COMPLEX

MIN : SEC

THE DIFFERENCES I SPOTTED

07 ○○○○○○○

SOLUTION ON PAGE 185

Pretty in blue

"When you fish for love, bait with your heart, not your brain."
— Mark Twain

COMPLEX

MIN : SEC

THE DIFFERENCES I SPOTTED

07

SOLUTION ON PAGE 185

Madame butterfly

According to the *Kwaidan: Stories and Studies of Strange Things*,
by Lafcadio Hearn, a butterfly symbolizes a person's soul
in all its different stages.

COMPLEX

MIN : SEC

SOLUTION ON PAGE 185

Coiled and cozy

Try and find the difference before our slithery friend wakes up.

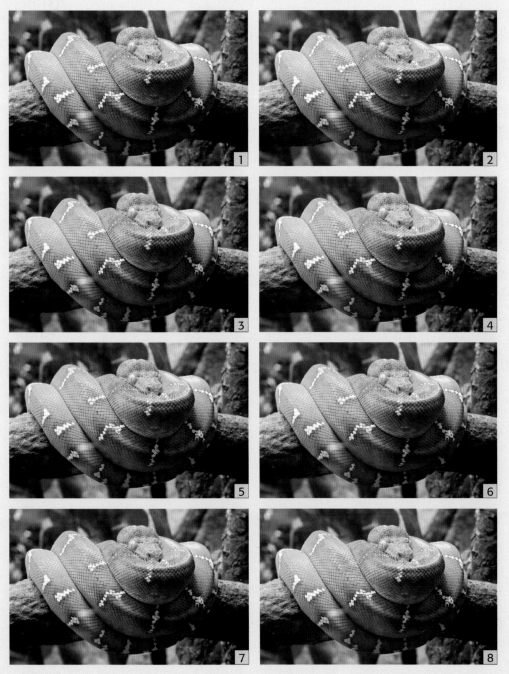

COMPLEX

MIN : SEC

SOLUTION ON PAGE 186

Berry blast!
Quick! Before this little one finishes his snack,
try and solve this puzzle.

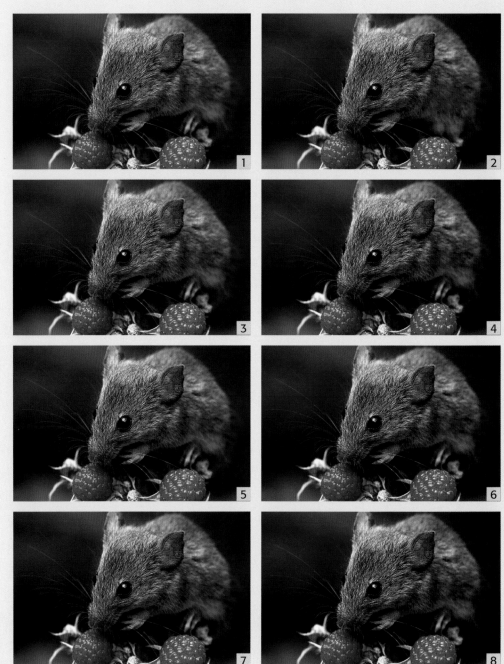

COMPLEX

MIN : SEC

SOLUTION ON PAGE 186

Snowy halo

The Goura Victoria is also known as the Victoria Crowned Pigeon, in honor of the British Queen Victoria of the UK.

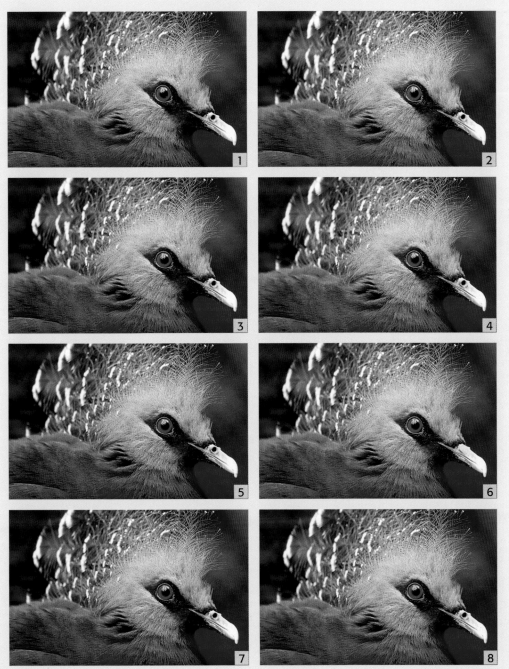

COMPLEX

MIN : SEC

SOLUTION ON PAGE 186

Just Ducky

While these ducks enjoy their winter wonderland, enjoy solving this mind-boggling puzzle!

DID YOU KNOW?
One of the species of duck that winters in Illinois, the Old Squaw is named so because of its noisy nature.

COMPLEX

MIN : SEC

THE DIFFERENCES I SPOTTED

10 ○○○○○○○○○○

SOLUTION ON PAGE 186

Bee silly!
Shredded bee larvae served with rice is a popular
Indonesian delicacy.

COMPLEX

MIN : SEC

THE DIFFERENCES I SPOTTED

08 ○○○○○○○○

SOLUTION ON PAGE 186

Lunch time!

Try and find all the differences between these two adorable images.

COMPLEX

MIN : SEC

THE DIFFERENCES I SPOTTED

08 ○○○○○○○○

SOLUTION ON PAGE 186

Burst of color down under

Coral colonies can live over 4,000 years. Dating back to the Bronze Age, the Leiopathes have been growing for 4,265 years.

COMPLEX

MIN : SEC

THE DIFFERENCES I SPOTTED

10 ○○○○○○○○○○

SOLUTION ON PAGE 187

Yes, deer!

All species of the male deer except for the Chinese Water Deer shed and then regrow their antlers annually.

COMPLEX

MIN : SEC

THE DIFFERENCES I SPOTTED

07 ○○○○○○○

SOLUTION ON PAGE 187

Waddle this way

Before this waddling bunch heads home, try and find all the differences between the two images.

COMPLEX

MIN : SEC

THE DIFFERENCES I SPOTTED

09 ○○○○○○○○○

SOLUTION ON PAGE 187

I'm swimming right at you
Before this fish nips you, quickly solve the puzzle.

COMPLEX

MIN : SEC

THE DIFFERENCES I SPOTTED

SOLUTION ON PAGE 187

Only fodder on my mind

You can tell the age of a cow by counting the number of rings on its horn.

COMPLEX

MIN : SEC

THE DIFFERENCES I SPOTTED

08 ○○○○○○○○

SOLUTION ON PAGE 187

The result of nature's creative moods
Even though these images look alike there are a few differences.

COMPLEX

MIN : SEC

THE DIFFERENCES I SPOTTED

SOLUTION ON PAGE 187

A purrfect pair
The White Tiger is not a separate subspecies of the tiger. The discoloration can occur in any species and is caused by a recessive gene.

COMPLEX

MIN : SEC

SOLUTION ON PAGE 188

The color in my life

The dusky leaf monkey is mainly found in Malaysia, southern Thailand, and Burma.

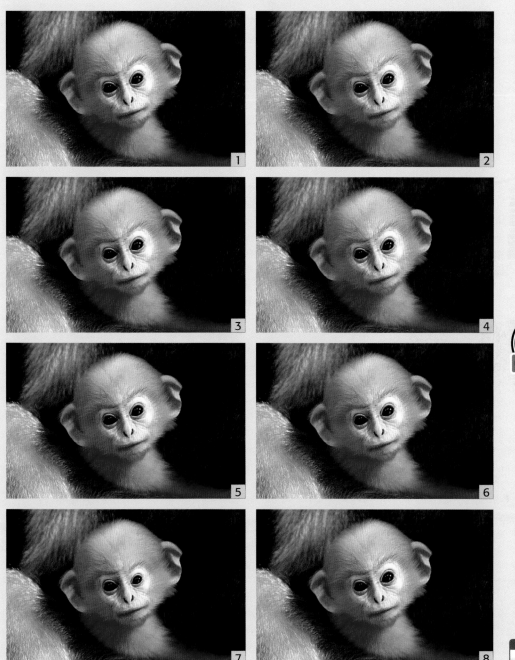

COMPLEX

MIN : SEC

SOLUTION ON PAGE 188

My little ballerina

While all these pups look as cute as one another, one of them stands out more than the rest. Can you spot it?

COMPLEX

MIN : SEC

SOLUTION ON PAGE 188

Friends forever

"A real friend is one who walks in when the rest of the world walks out." — Walter Winchell

COMPLEX

MIN : SEC

SOLUTION ON PAGE 188

Full speed ahead

Wildebeest is actually Dutch for "wild beast." In Tanzania they are also known as *gnus*.

DID YOU KNOW?
When wildebeest cross rivers and other obstacles they do so as one; this is known as "swarm intelligence."

COMPLEX

MIN : SEC

THE DIFFERENCES I SPOTTED

10 ○○○○○○○○○○

SOLUTION ON PAGE 188

Off to school!

Before this school of fish get to school, try and find all the differences between these two pictures.

COMPLEX

MIN : SEC

THE DIFFERENCES I SPOTTED

09 ○○○○○○○○○

SOLUTION ON PAGE 188

Jumping jacks of the sea

In terms of diet, all dolphins are carnivores.

COMPLEX

MIN : SEC

THE DIFFERENCES I SPOTTED

SOLUTION ON PAGE 189

Parrot talk

Before this pretty lot flies home, find all the differences between the images.

COMPLEX

MIN : SEC

THE DIFFERENCES I SPOTTED

09 ○○○○○○○○○

SOLUTION ON PAGE 189

Who're you calling a chicken?

Without getting your feathers ruffled, try and find all the differences between these two images.

COMPLEX

MIN : SEC

THE DIFFERENCES I SPOTTED

SOLUTION ON PAGE 189

Time to come together

Until 10,000 years ago, lions were the most widespread
mammals on the planet, second only to human beings.

COMPLEX

MIN : SEC

THE DIFFERENCES I SPOTTED

08 ○○○○○○○○

SOLUTION ON PAGE 189

A chick chick here! A chick chick there!

Before Mama Hen takes her babies home, try and find all the differences between the images.

COMPLEX

MIN : SEC

THE DIFFERENCES I SPOTTED

SOLUTION ON PAGE 189

In a while crocodile!
The most dangerous crocodiles are the Nile and the Australian crocodiles.

COMPLEX

MIN : SEC

THE DIFFERENCES I SPOTTED

07 ○○○○○○○

SOLUTION ON PAGE 189

Uniqueness personified

"No one can possibly achieve any real and lasting success or 'get rich' in business by being a conformist." — J. Paul Getty

COMPLEX

MIN : SEC

THE DIFFERENCES I SPOTTED

SOLUTION ON PAGE 190

Our own waterfall!

Before the party ends, try and find all the differences
between the two images.

COMPLEX

MIN : SEC

THE DIFFERENCES I SPOTTED

09 ○○○○○○○○○

SOLUTION ON PAGE 190

Chick-a-dee! Chick-a-doo!

The two images look alike. However, if you look carefully, you can spot the differences.

COMPLEX

MIN : SEC

THE DIFFERENCES I SPOTTED

08 ○○○○○○○○○

SOLUTION ON PAGE 190

A pair of Pradas would be nice

While these cats get some shut eye in the Sun, try and find all the differences between these images.

COMPLEX

MIN : SEC

THE DIFFERENCES I SPOTTED

08 ○○○○○○○○○

SOLUTION ON PAGE 190

Where are you all going?

While this baby elephant tries to convince his family to go swimming, see if you can spot all the differences between the two images.

COMPLEX

MIN : SEC

THE DIFFERENCES I SPOTTED

09

SOLUTION ON PAGE 190

No winter coat for me!
Spread over 20,000 farms, the Dutch sheep population
is estimated to be 1.5 million.

COMPLEX

MIN : SEC

THE DIFFERENCES I SPOTTED

10 ○○○○○○○○○○

SOLUTION ON PAGE 190

A true romantic

"You don't marry someone you can live with, you marry the person you can't live without." — Unknown Source

COMPLEX

MIN : SEC

THE DIFFERENCES I SPOTTED

07 ○○○○○○○

SOLUTION ON PAGE 191

It's your turn to find the ball

While these puppies search for the ball, try and look for
all the differences between these two images.

COMPLEX

MIN : SEC

THE DIFFERENCES I SPOTTED

06 ○○○○○○

SOLUTION ON PAGE 191

Rush hour

Try and solve this puzzle before they reach the other side.

PHOTO FUN PICTURE PUZZLES—ANIMALS

COMPLEX

MIN : SEC

THE DIFFERENCES I SPOTTED

09 ○○○○○○○○○

SOLUTION ON PAGE 191

I'm no chicken!
Beat the clock and quickly spot the odd image.

COMPLEX

MIN : SEC

SOLUTION ON PAGE 191

Springtime
"If nothing ever changed there would be no butterflies."
— Unknown Source

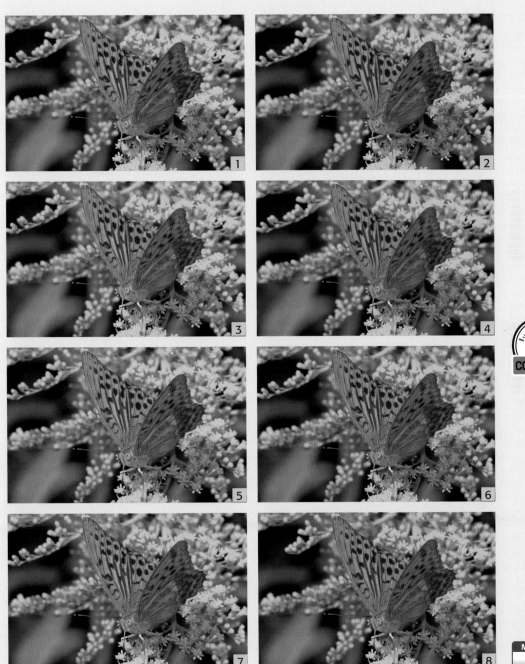

COMPLEX

MIN : SEC

SOLUTION ON PAGE 191

Walking tall

The Swahili name for giraffe is "twiga."

COMPLEX

MIN : SEC

SOLUTION ON PAGE 191

Let's not get nosy!
Baby seals are playful creatures and actually enjoy being tickled under their "arms."

COMPLEX

MIN : SEC

SOLUTION ON PAGE 192

Page 09:

Page 10:

Page 11:

Page 12:

Page 13:

Page 14:

Page 15:

Page 16:

Page 17:

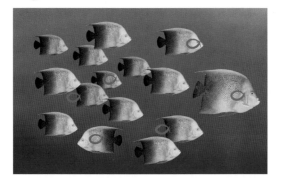

Page 18:

Page 19:

Page 20:

Page 21:

Page 23:

Page 24:

Page 25:

Page 26:

Page 27:

Page 28:

Page 29:

Page 30:

Page 31:

Page 32:

Page 33:

ANSWERS

Page 34:

Page 35:

Page 37:

Page 38:

Page 39:

Page 40:

Page 41:

Page 42:

Page 43:

Page 44:

Page 45:

Page 46:

Page 47:

Page 49:

Page 50:

Page 51:

Page 52:

Page 53:

Page 54:

Page 55:

Page 56:

Page 57:

Page 58:

Page 59:

Page 60:

Page 61:

Page 65:

Page 66:

Page 67:

Page 68:

Page 69:

Page 70:

Page 71:

Page 72:

Page 73:

Page 74:

Page 75:

Page 77:

Page 78:

Page 79:

Page 80:

Page 81:

Page 82:

Page 83:

Page 84:

Page 85:

Page 86:

Page 87:

Page 89:

Page 90:

Page 91:

Page 92:

Page 93:

Page 94:

Page 95:

Page 96:

Page 97:

Page 98:

Page 99:

Page 101:

Page 102:

Page 103:

Page 104:

Page 105:

Page 106:

Page 107:

Page 108:

Page 109:

Page 110:

Page 111:

Page 112:

Page 113:

Page 114:

Page 115:

Page 116:

Page 117:

Page 121:

Page 122:

Page 123:

Page 124:

Page 125:

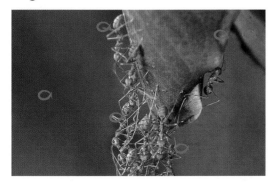

Page 126:

Page 127:

Page 128:

Page 129:

Page 130:

Page 131:

Page 133:

Page 134:

Page 135:

Page 136:

Page 137:

Page 138:

Page 139:

Page 140:

Page 141:

Page 142:

Page 143:

Page 144:

Page 145:

Page 147:

Page 148:

Page 149:

Page 150:

Page 151:

Page 152:

Page 153:

Page 154:

Page 155:

Page 156:

Page 157:

Page 158:

Page 159:

Page 160:

Page 161:

Page 162:

Page 163:

Page 164:

Page 165:

Page 166:

Page 167: